SOUL SALVATION

The Salvation of the mind

By Pastor Elizabeth J. Smither

SOUL SALVATION: The Salvation of the Mind

ISBN 10: 0-9726797-1-5
ISBN 13: 978-0-9726797-1-8
Copyright © 2014 by Elizabeth J. Smither
122 East Broadway St.
Frankfort, KY 40601

Published by:
Times of Refreshing Publishing
122 East Broadway St.
Frankfort, KY 40601
502-875-7886

Printed in the United States of America.
All rights reserved under International Copyright Law. Contents and/or cover may not be reproduced in whole or in part in any form without the express written consent of the Publisher.

All Scripture quotations are taken from the New King James Bible c 1979 by Thomas Nelson, Inc.

Acknowledgements

With deep gratitude I acknowledge Dr. Ron Callahan and Dr. Philip D. Derber for introducing and teaching me about the dividing of soul and spirit and secondly for praying me through many tests which proved the validity of this revelation. Of course, I am most thankful to my husband, Fantley, and sons with whom I have had many long discussions and with whom we have lived out many parables and testimonies.

In Appreciation

For Dudley J. Conner and all who appreciate the understanding of the different realms of spirit and soul. We, as well as he, looked so forward to our many discussions.

TABLE OF CONTENTS

Preface   7

Chapter One   9
Where is The Battleground?

Chapter Two   17
Who is Ruling The House?

Chapter Three   27
The Rhythm of Faith

Chapter Four   39
Poet the Word

Chapter Five   45
Air Traffic Controller

Chapter Six   53
A Holy Day

Chapter Seven   63
Tourniquets in the Soul

Chapter Eight   69
Covenant Bridge

Chapter Nine   79
Guard the Garden

Chapter Ten   85
Oxymoron

Preface

In ministry the root of most confusion and lack of victory in the Body of Christ has been a lack of knowledge concerning the dividing of soul and spirit. The fact that you <u>are</u> a spirit and <u>have</u> a soul has not been understood in the Body of Christ as a whole. I Thessalonians 5:23 states,

**Now may the God of peace
Himself sanctify you completely;
and may your whole spirit, soul,
and body be preserved blameless
at the coming of our Lord Jesus
Christ.**

The essence of this study is to help the believer identify the soul arena as being different from the real you—spirit. This enables the disciple to be more objective about the fight of faith and to renew their mind and manifest the victory that Jesus bought for us.

**For the word of God is living and powerful, and sharper than any two-edged sword, piercing even to the division of soul and spirit, joints and marrow, and is a discerner of the thoughts and intents of the heart.
Hebrews 4:12**

**… Do not be conformed to this world, but be transformed by the renewing of your mind, that you may prove what is the good and acceptable and perfect will of God.
Romans 12:2**

CHAPTER ONE
Where is the Battleground?

"Why is it that I do not always feel saved?" "Why do attacks of oppression and depression still exist?" "If I am seated in heavenly places in Christ Jesus, what is this fight of faith all about?" "If we are far above all principality and power, why are we instructed to 'war a good warfare,' according to 1 Timothy 1:18?" Enter soul world revelation!

Remember General Braddock's British army in the beginning stages of the French and Indian war? His battle plan gives us a mental picture of how unprepared for the fight we as Christians have been in the past. **My people are destroyed for lack of knowledge** (Hosea 4:6). The British in their bright red and white uniforms were trained to fight in the open fields of Europe. When they went marching off into the American wilderness looking for the battlefield, they were easy targets for the French and Indians who were hiding behind trees and rocks. Even though the British had the latest and best in weaponry, skilled and schooled leadership, and well-trained ranks they were hopelessly routed because they could not locate the battlefield!

The church has all of heaven's reserves including

myriads of angels on our side, the Blood of Christ speaking better than the blood of Abel, Jesus at the right hand of God making intercession for us, the Holy Spirit making intercession for us, even the creation itself in earnest expectation waiting for the manifestation of the sons of God—and yet the church is just "hanging on" until Jesus comes back, oblivious to its position of strength and power. For the most part the church is full of people who are depressed, sick, and barely making ends meet from one paycheck to the next. Some of the most profitable businesses are pharmaceutical companies —right here in the wealthiest nation on the planet where a high percentage of the population claim to be Christian. Where is the battlefield? The church is marching through the wilderness all dressed up looking for the battlefield and providing an easy target for oppression, fear, terror, sickness, infirmities, and poverty.

To answer these and other questions, we must take a closer look into the Word of God concerning the anatomy of the unseen world. First of all, you are spirit. In John 4:24 we read, **God is spirit, and those who worship Him must worship Him in spirit and in truth.** In other words, in order to commune and communicate with God, we must accomplish this in the spiritual, unseen realm. God would not require us to do something that was impossible to do, so we must be spiritual beings—with a decision to make. Are we going to worship Him (as He has declared we must) in spirit, or attempt to contact God some other way? 1 John 3:2 declares, **Beloved, now we are children of God...** When are we the children of God? Now! That is <u>not</u> when we get to heaven. Children always carry their father's image. We are essentially spirit beings. God is spirit. We are born again of God. He is our Father. We are spirit.

Let's look at a couple of other scriptures which will shed more light on our 'unseen realm' anatomy. In Hebrews 4:12 we read, **For the Word of God is living and powerful, and sharper than any two-edged sword, piercing even to the division of soul and spirit...** Did you see that—soul <u>and</u> spirit! Also, 1 Thessalonians 5:23 says, **Now may the God of peace Himself sanctify you completely; and may your whole spirit, soul and body be preserved blameless at the coming of our Lord Jesus Christ.** It says spirit AND soul. We know that the physical body is not a part of the invisible realm; so we need not discuss that at this time. But what about spirit and soul? It is obvious from the passage in Hebrews 4:12 that spirit and soul are so closely linked or so similar that it takes something special to differentiate between the two. The Word of God is described as "sharper than any two-edged sword," so sharp in fact that it can even divide soul and spirit. Soul and spirit must be very tightly linked. But, even as tightly linked as they are, they <u>can</u> be divided even if the Word of God is the only agent able to do so.

We know that you are spirit, born again it says in 1 Peter 1:23 **...of the incorruptible seed of God's Word, made in His image, in His likeness--sons of God.** But what about the soul? Is it the same as spirit? Is it a separate entity that works closely with the spirit? If the Word of God can divide soul and spirit, then by the Word of God we must be able to describe or discern the difference between soul and spirit.

Ask any woman who has given birth, *"Was there ever a time when you were almost pregnant or perhaps halfway pregnant or maybe 'kind of' pregnant?"* Of course not! When a woman is with child, it is an accomplished fact, with no ifs, ands, or buts. It is what some would call a 'done deal.' So it is with the born again spirit. Romans 10:9 states, **that if you confess with your mouth the Lord Jesus and believe in your heart that God has raised Him from the dead, you will be saved.** Following that, 1 Peter 1:23 says, **having been born again, not of corruptible seed but of incorruptible, through the Word of God which lives and abides forever.** The first scripture indicates a conditional promise from God, that if you do that, this will happen. However, the second scripture states that once the condition is met, the end result is not just halfway accomplished, just 'sort of' born again; no, a birthing has happened inside you. It's a 'done deal.' You are born again of God's seed, a child of God.

However when we investigate the scriptures dealing with the soul, we find something quite different. The book of James is a pastoral letter written by James to his flock—people who are born again and are children of God. Even though they are born-again spirits they are dealing with certain temptations or trials in their Christian lives. But look at verse 1:21b, **...and receive with meekness the implanted word, which is able to save your souls.** *"Is able"* implies a continuing agency; yet he is writing to born again 'done deal' people whom he addresses in verse two as *"my brethren."* In Paul's epistle to the Philippian church (who are called saints in verse one and are in partnership with Paul) he writes in chapter 2 verse 12b, **...work out your own salvation with fear and trembling.** Also Peter in the ninth verse of 1 Peter chapter one exhorts these born again spirits in **receiving the end of your faith—the salvation of *your* souls.** Again in Heb 10:39 **But we are not of those who draw back to perdition, but of those who believe to the saving of the soul.**

This discussion of the division of soul and spirit can easily be settled using the scripture in Romans chapter 12:2, **And do not be conformed to this world, but be transformed by the renewing of your mind...** Focus on that phrase *"be transformed."* The original Greek text is interesting. The word in the Greek for transformed is *metamorphomai.* That is the root word from which we get our English word metamorphosis. Metamorphosis is the process by which a caterpillar is transformed into a butterfly.

A caterpillar can be very destructive and not the kind of beautiful pet that would be in most people's dreams. Yet once it has spun around itself a shelter, a chrysalis (sometimes called a cocoon), a marvelous transformation begins. It may appear from the outside that nothing is happening. It may even look dead. But within that chrysalis a metamorphosis is happening. A butterfly is developing. That ugly, nondescript worm will break forth from its apparently lifeless habitation in the form of a beautiful, winged creature that is no longer limited to ground level maneuvering. It has become an expression of beauty and liberty. The scripture commands us to *be transformed*—to undergo metamorphosis. How can that happen? A beautiful, liberating metamorphosis will happen when you determine to renew your mind with the truths of God's goodness. In other words, you can wrap up your mind, spin a cocoon, with God's Word. And what will result? A metamorphosis will happen. Areas of your life which in the past have not been very beautiful or elegant will be transformed into something wonderful!

What we have in view is a process that happens continually and brings a future result. We are dealing with the mind, which is a separate entity from the 'done deal' spiritual birthing. In dealing with the mind in this way, a marvelous transformation can result which brings the beauty of the spirit realm, where God abides, into this natural, earthy existence. Are you seeing a correlation between this scripture in Romans 12:2 and the passages in James 1:21 and 1 Peter 1:9? **...Be transformed by the renewing of you mind... receiving the end of your faith—the salvation of your souls.** And look again at James 1:21: **...receive with meekness the implanted word, which is able to save your souls.** Could we not make some reasonable substitutions in the previous passages to get even more understanding? Try this, *be transformed by the salvation of your soul.* Or look at this, *...receive the Word implanted which is able to renew your mind for a transformation.*

Before we go further, I want to make a very simple yet profound and vitally important point. The mind is an exceptional mechanism which is capable of being renewed by any number of streams of information. It can be renewed to various rules and regulations concerning a sport (which would enable a person to be transformed out of ignorance into an adept player). It can be renewed to computer technology or a card game. It can be renewed to soap operas and romantic novels. Whatever discipline a person decides to pursue, the mind is capable of mastering. The mind must be renewed to a particular body of information in order for that person to be competent in a new area of expertise. The choice is yours. All the previously named examples are natural, earthy disciplines. What would happen if a people chose to renew their minds with supernatural information? Could it be possible for that people to live a supernatural lifestyle?

In the age in which we live, many books and tapes are available with spiritual information that may or may not help in the transformation process. It is the focus of this book to seek the highest form of transformation possible. Only Jesus Christ of Nazareth came to bring salvation to a corrupt world. Only Jesus became a curse to redeem us from the curse of poverty, sickness and disease, grief and infirmity. In Jesus Christ, we have more than 'heaven insurance'. In John 10:10 Jesus says, **...I have come that they may have life, and that they may have it more abundantly.** And that is what this book is all about, namely, living the abundant life through the salvation or transformation of the mind. That is soul salvation.

CHAPTER TWO
Who is ruling the house?

Not too long ago I went to visit a friend of mine who had very active small children. Just as we would begin a conversation, one of the children would need some attention. By the time we returned to the conversation, we had either forgotten what we were talking about or the topic was re-directed. We would try again, but it seemed as soon as the child was no longer the center of attention, he would do something that would demand attention. What was unusual and seemed out of place was that the adult friend was not teaching the children discipline. Who was ruling the house? The children seemed to be in charge.

No one would have difficulty recognizing this household as being out of order. But what about the house or temple of your body in which you dwell? Are you being ruled by your emotions? Does information from your five physical senses dictate your every decision and every move? Proverbs 3:5-6 states, **...lean not on your own understanding; In all your ways acknowledge Him, and He shall direct your paths.** Are you, spirit, in control; or is your mind or emotions ruling the house? Remember, you are spirit. You have a mind and emotions.

Some things God asks you to do may not make sense to your mind at first. For instance, you find a promise in the Word of God concerning giving. God says the way to have financial increase is to give.

> **Give, and it will be given to you: good measure, pressed down, shaken together, and running over will be put into your bosom... Luke 6:38**

> **...He who sows bountifully will also reap bountifully. 2 Corinthians 9:6**

> **"Bring all the tithes into the storehouse, that there may be food in My house, And try Me now in this," Says the Lord of Hosts, "If I will not open for you the windows of heaven and pour out for you *such* blessing that *there will* not *be room* enough to *receive it*" Malachi 3:10**

The worldly system and the system that may seem right to the mind is to acquire all that you can and save it. Is your way of doing things being dominated by what seems right to the mind or by what God's Word says? Are you going to believe God's Word or *"lean to your own understanding?"* If you are being ruled by your mind and emotions, you are being dominated by your primary child. The child (your soul) is 'calling the shots,' not you, spirit.

Look at Psalm 131:2. **Surely I have calmed and quieted my soul, Like a weaned child with his mother; Like a weaned child is my soul within me.** Just as a child needs discipline, correction, direction, and teaching, so does your soul. In Galatians 4:1-2 we read**, ...the heir, as long as he is a child, does not differ at all from a slave, though he is master of all, but is under guardians and stewards until the time appointed by the Father.**

Several years ago an inner city school had an interesting situation occur. All around the school play yard was a high fence that was the boundary for the children's play. But it not only acted as a boundary; the children would also climb on it, bounce off of it, throw balls against it, and otherwise incorporate it into their activities. At some point, the authorities decided the children did not really need the fence. They were concerned that it hindered their free spirit. That, somehow the fence might make them feel like caged animals and keep them from having liberty in their minds and thought processes. So, down came the fence; and what was the result? Instead of using the whole play yard as they had been doing, parameters and all, they concentrated their play toward the center of the playground. The fence actually had given the children a sense of security and protection that increased their liberty instead of stifling it.

The same could be said of your mind and emotions, your soul. Left undisciplined with no boundaries or 'fence', feelings of insecurity will abound. That soul will either be so overwhelmed by fear that it will not allow you to try anything new, or it will try anything desperately looking for 'meaning to life.' You are responsible for your soul, to discipline it, train it, correct it, and direct it in the right path. A soul that is disciplined in the ways and thoughts of God will allow the spirit to have liberty.

Take a moment to recall once again the triune being that you are. You have a physical body. That part is easy. It's your tent, your temple; some call it your earth suit. To have authority and do anything in this physical realm, you must have an earth suit. You can judge that part of you with your five physical senses. But there is also an unseen part that cannot be judged in that same way. Many characteristics of that unseen part of you can be known through actions and reactions in the physical body; but as far as actually seeing with the physical eyes that invisible part of you, it is just that—invisible. And as we have stated before, even that invisible part of you can be divided into two main parts—spirit and soul. Hebrews 4:12 says, **For the word of God is living and powerful, and sharper than any two-edged sword, piercing even to the division of soul and spirit...** Now watch this carefully. In Colossians 2:11 the scripture states, **In Him you were also circumcised with the circumcision made without hands, by putting off the body of the sins of the flesh, by the circumcision of Christ.** In Romans 2:29 we see that circumcision is that of the heart, the spiritual heart, not the mind or emotions. We also see in Colossians 2:15 that Christ, **Having disarmed principalities and powers, He made a public spectacle of them, triumphing over them in it.** Yet in

Hebrews 10:12-13 He says, **But this man, after He had offered one sacrifice for sins forever, sat down at the right hand of God, from that time waiting till His enemies are made His footstool.**

In other passages, a similar dichotomy exists. Hebrews 9:23 shows us that the heavenly things themselves were cleansed with better sacrifices than the blood of animals, namely the blood of Jesus Christ Himself. Yet in II Timothy 4:7 Paul says that he had **...fought the good fight...** and in Ephesians 6:12 that, **...we do not wrestle against flesh and blood...** In Luke 10:19 Jesus says He has given His disciples authority over all the power of the enemy. Yet I Peter 5:8 states that we should, **Be sober, be vigilant; because your adversary the devil walks about like a roaring lion, seeking whom he may devour.**

You are a new creation in Christ Jesus, born again in your spirit by the incorruptible seed of God's Word. The spirit realm has been cleansed by the blood of Jesus, and Satan has been cast down from heaven. But there exists another unseen realm where the battlefield is located. It is that mental, psychological, emotional realm that I call the soul world. Your adversary, satan, is called in Ephesians 2:2 **the prince of the power of the air.** He has tried to set up his kingdom in that unseen atmospheric, thought realm and attempted to make it look spiritual. He is a fallen spirit confined to the psychological, feeling realm. He has no physical body and thus has no authority in this physical realm unless he can pressure someone with an earth suit to talk and act like him. The battlefield is not in the spiritual world, not in the physical world but in the soul world.

Remember, you are spirit, seated in heavenly places in Christ Jesus. But you have a mind and you have emotions. You are not your mind. Your mind is full of temporal information, that is, information that can be changed. You—spirit—are eternal, made in God's image, a son of God. You—spirit—can grow, develop and mature in the things of God. The mind, however, must be changed, renewed, washed, and delivered into higher spiritual reality.

Romans 12:2 instructs us to be transformed by the renewing of our minds. Actually the Greek word for soul is *psuche* where we get our word psychology and various other words related to the mind and the study of it. The will or 'chooser,' can be thought of as being in the center of the mind. For instance, God speaks in Deuteronomy 30:19 of choices that must be made by an individual. **I call heaven and earth as witnesses today against you, *that* I have set before you life and death, blessing and cursing; therefore choose life...** Romans 8:6 says, **For to be carnally minded is death, but to be spiritually minded is life and peace.** In other words, whatever a person has focused his mind on and renewed his mind to will determine what choices he will make. If the mind is renewed with things of the spirit, the individual will choose life. If the mind is renewed with information of the natural realm, the individual will more than likely choose death, perhaps without even knowing that is what he or she is choosing. Essentially, that is how a person can be *"transformed by the renewing of the mind."* When the mind is renewed with the information that God

Himself is seeing and saying, it enables that individual to **...not look at the things which are seen, but at the things which are not seen** (2 Corinthians 4:18). It is then that the person begins making choices according to and in agreement with what the Spirit is saying. The course of that person's life is changed to be in conformity with the born again spirit that longs to have outward expression!

We must see the soul as a separate entity which must be saved or delivered into higher spiritual reality. **Receive with meekness the implanted word, which is able to save your souls** (James 1:21). Realize that the *"spirit is born again"* while the *"soul is saved."* Such scriptures as 1 Peter 1:9 are now more understandable: **receiving the end of your faith—even the salvation of your souls.** And Philippians 2:12 **...work out your own** (soul) **salvation with fear and trembling**. Although the born again spirit is an immediate work, the salvation of the soul is a gradual process. **Therefore, if anyone is in Christ,** *he is* **a new creation; old things have passed away; behold, all things have become new** (2 Corinthians 5:17). Notice the *"have become"* in the previous passage. The spirit is born again and the soul is saved as the mind is renewed. This results in natural circumstances being transformed and reflecting spiritual truth. Even one's outward appearance can be affected.

THE COMPUTER MIND

Think of the mind as your computer. It is the best computer that exists; even so, it's a computer nonetheless. When a person is born again, a newly created spirit is birthed inside that person. **Therefore, if**

anyone is in Christ, he is a new creation... (2 Corinthians 5:17). A new person who never existed before has come alive! I have new life, a new beginning, and I am not the same person I was. There is only one problem: the mind, will, and emotions and the physical body are the same. Here is a new person with the former soul which inhabits the former body. The new creation in the innermost being will never express itself until the mind is renewed to who that new person is in Christ Jesus. In other words, that computer mind must be reprogrammed with spiritual information concerning the new person who is complete in Christ Jesus.

Previously that computer mind was programmed carnally according to the course of this world, which is full of fear. When the computer mind is reprogrammed spiritually according to what God says about you, you will choose the things of faith, and victory will manifest in every area of your life. **...this is the victory that has overcome the world—our faith** (I John 5:4). **Beloved, I pray that you may prosper in all things and be in health, just as your SOUL** (emphasis added) **prospers** (3 John 2). We could restate that by saying that you will prosper and be in health even as your computer mind is reprogrammed with spiritual information that will cause you to choose life. Can you see that prosperity and health are part of your divine nature—that new creation that God has birthed inside you? And how does that new creation have expression in this natural realm? **...Be transformed by the renewing of your mind...** (Romans 12:2).

Now let's go back to Braddock's army. Why was his

army put to shame and routed when it seemingly had all the advantages over the enemy? Because they did not know where the battle would be fought. Why is the church as a whole not prospering and in health according to the provision that we have in Christ Jesus? Because we have not known where the battlefield is located. Is the battlefield in the spiritual realm? No, the battlefield is in the soul world. The Promised Land that we are to possess is the soul, especially the mind. **By your patience POSSESS your souls** (Luke 21:19).

CHAPTER THREE
The Rhythm of Faith

You are spirit. If you have received Jesus Christ as your Lord and Savior, you are born again (literally, born from above) in your spirit. You have a mind, will and emotions; and you live in that physical body here on the earth. In the last chapter we discussed the fact that your mind requires renewing or reprogramming. Just as a caterpillar must spin a chrysalis (cocoon) to be transformed into a butterfly, you must wrap your mind up with the Word of God to allow the real you—spirit—to have expression in this natural realm. The caterpillar has all the genetic coding of a butterfly within itself; but without the chrysalis phase of its life, it will never accomplish that butterfly potential. It will always be a destructive worm, limited to the 'beggarly elements' of ground travel, with no real beauty that comes from the inside out.

The most practical method that I have found to feed my spirit and renew my mind is a rhythm of faith. As we go over the elements of this rhythm, keep in mind that a little amount every day consistently is better than a lot sporadically.

Proverbs 13:4 says that the soul of the diligent is

made fat. Consider this analogy. If a young ox has a lightweight wooden yoke placed around its neck and that yoke is never altered or removed but the ox is still fed and continues to grow, what do you think will happen to the yoke? As the ox is fed properly and continues to grow, suddenly the pressure of that growth process will be too much for the yoke. It will be broken. The yoke will be destroyed because of fatness. Of course, the more you apply yourself to this rhythm—as long as it is consistent—the faster the desired result will manifest.

These guidelines are by no means exhaustive, but will form a foundation for establishing your own criteria for spinning your chrysalis. One of the most important elements of this rhythm is what I call soul exercises. A runner does not just decide he is going to jump out on the track and run an Olympic race without exercising and training. Just as the physical body requires discipline and exercise to be toned and capable of performing, so also the soul.

When you were awakened this morning did someone have to remind you what your name is, where you live, what color eyes you have, etc.? Of course not! You have an awareness of these natural facts no matter how you feel. If the facts of your address and eye color are imprinted so firmly, (conditions which are natural, temporal, subject to change) how much more should we be constantly aware of eternal facts? Did you awaken aware of the new creation inside you? Did you awaken aware that you are the righteousness of God in Christ Jesus? 2 Corinthians 5:21 says, **For He made Him who knew no sin *to be* sin for us, that we might become the**

righteousness of God in Him.

When did we become righteous in our spirit—in right standing with God? When we received Jesus as Lord. We are born again as a righteous, new creation. If that awareness is not present, then it is time for some mind wrapping and soul exercising. I suggest you make your own list of scriptures that will help establish that awareness and keep the soul disciplined, focused, and armed. If your mind seems unwilling to receive the reality of the born again righteous nature, or if symptoms of unrighteous behavior, lack, or oppression persist, triple the dosage. You cannot overdose on the Word of God and the side effects are all good.

When your soul comes to attention and becomes aware of spiritual reality, the second item on this list is praise. Psalm 22:3 says that God inhabits the praises of His people. What better way is there to seek God in a regular rhythm of faith than to have your atmosphere charged with His presence? Practicing the presence of God is most beneficial for your spirit, soul, and body. This praise time can be done through the agent of music or simply in words from your heart, releasing thanksgiving to God for who He is to you. *"You are my Refuge, my strong tower, and my deliverer. You are my Fortress, my rock, my Righteousness, my Sanctification, and my Redemption. You are my Wisdom, my Illumination, my Revelation, my blood kinsman Redeemer. You are my Healer, my Restoration, my exceeding great Reward, my Rewarder, my Alpha and Omega, my Captain of the hosts and King of kings and Lord of lords."*

Once you start this good habit, there is no end to the revelation of who He is to you. Every day you can hear more. After a praise session there is a good atmosphere in which to pray faith filled prayers for your family, the leadership of the church and your co-workers (in the body and otherwise). A session of praise every day will keep you ahead of most prayer 'emergencies' that could arise.

In John 10:10, Jesus states: **The thief does not come except to steal, and to kill, and to destroy. I have come that they might have life, and that they may have *it* more abundantly.** The devil, the adversary, who is walking about seeking whom he may devour (1 Peter 5:8), is the life taker. Jesus is the life giver. If we only pray for people in need or for their needs, are we not being led in our prayer life by the devil instead of the Spirit of Faith? *"Well, the doctors say Uncle Alfred has been under too much oppression at work and that caused him to have a heart attack. Okay, let's pray for Uncle Alfred." "Well, cousin Suzie fell asleep at the wheel and wrecked her car. Let's pray for cousin Suzie." "We don't know what happened to Charlie. He just snapped and ended up in a mental hospital. We had better pray for Charlie."* Now who do you think is the instigator of the oppression at work, the overly tired Suzie and the pressure that has caused that mental collapse? I am not saying you shouldn't pray for these individuals. It is recorded in Acts 10:38 that Jesus Himself went about **... healing all who were oppressed by the devil...** But if that is the only kind of praying you do, who is directing your prayer time? Perhaps in a regular rhythm of faith, in the midst of our thanksgiving to God we pray for Uncle Alfred to access more of God's grace at work, that he would be established in righteousness and oppression would be far from him (Isaiah 54:14). In a consistent way, we can pray for Suzie to be strengthened with might by His Spirit in the inner man (Ephesians 3:16). Being led by His presence in prayer, we may receive wisdom so that Charlie can avoid a mental breakdown. Would not praying in a regular rhythm of faith be more led of His Holy Spirit than just praying for needs originated by an unholy spirit?

It is critical to spend time praying for yourself. If you have the baptism of the Spirit with the evidence of speaking in tongues, this is a good opportunity to use that gift. If not, simply spend some time asking God to reveal His Word to you. Jesus remarks in Matthew 13:11 that, **...it has been given to you to know the mysteries of the kingdom of heaven...** Ask Him to reveal those mysteries. Ask for, **the spirit of wisdom and revelation in the knowledge of Him, the eyes of your understanding being enlightened...** (Ephesians 1:17, 18). Seek Him and talk to Him as **a friend who sticks closer than a brother** (Proverbs 18:24).

Then open the Word of God. If you have no immediate leading, start with the Proverb for the day. It says in the book of Proverbs chapter one that these proverbs are **to know wisdom and instruction, to perceive the words of understanding.** In other words, in the Proverbs you will find keys of knowledge that will unlock pathways of understanding for the rest of the Bible. There is one Proverb for each day of the month.

It will give you something to think about all day.

The last of the guidelines we will discuss has to do with an exercise I call 'juicing the Word'. Think of what happens with a vegetable juicer. On a regular 'rhythm' of eating, you can only consume a certain amount of vegetables. But with a juicer, you can take all those vegetables, put them through the juicer, drink that juice in a few minutes and take in all the benefits, vitamins, minerals, and other nutrients, in a much smaller amount of time.

> **For as the rain comes down, and the snow from heaven, and do not return there, but water the earth, and make it bring forth and bud, that it may give seed to the sower and bread to the eater, so shall My Word be that goes forth from My mouth; it shall not return to Me void, but it shall accomplish what I please, and it shall prosper *in the thing* for which I sent it.**
> **Isaiah 55:10,11**

Juicing the Word is a marvelous way to train the mind to focus. Remember, the battle is in the realm of the soul (mind, will, and emotions). When the battle is on, it is difficult to focus enough in the Word of God to feed your spirit, the real you. Anything we receive from God, we receive by faith. The adversary, the defeated devil, tries to disconnect a person from his relationship with God so that he will not feed his spirit. Faith is spiritual;

and it must be fed to stand strong. The enemy tries to bring distraction to the mind to hinder focus. Without focus, it is difficult to commune with the Holy Spirit and feed on the Word.

In juicing the Word of God, a person is taking chapters, passages, and even whole books of the Bible (being led of the Spirit) and meditating and memorizing the scripture in context. Committing to this discipline always gets a person beyond distractions. Feeding on the Word of God strengthens the spirit for the battle. It gets the soul above the parade and keeps the fruit of the spirit flowing.

Secondly, juicing the Word in this way keeps the focus of revelation on that Word and enhances understanding of that particular word in the context of that passage. When a scripture is taken out of context and put with other scriptures that seem similar there is often a twisting or a lack of clarity which results. This is avoided by working with the scriptures in context, meditating and memorizing.

Thirdly, meditating and memorizing passages in context brings a person into progressive and deeper revelation of the Word. Even though the flesh may desire to skip a particular verse or two, the temptation is avoided by 'plowing up fallow ground' in context. This is a process I call sub-soiling. To aerate the soil, and to bring up deeply imbedded rocks for removal, a farmer will dig deeper into the soil with a special plow. It allows roots to go deeper and grow stronger.

Juicing in context works in this manner: the first verse is worked, meditated and memorized the first day.

Then the next day, go over the first verse, meditating and adding another verse. The third day go over the first and second verses meditating and adding another. By the fifth day, the scriptures that were worked the first day begin to mean more and a deeper understanding starts developing. Staying with it even up to starting from the first verse several months later will bring up rocks of unbelief, offense, and wrong understanding. Once these rocks are brought out and dealt with, a deeper relationship with the Holy Spirit in His Word ensues. There is no limit to His understanding.

What may take hours of reading to properly feed your spirit is accomplished in a short amount of time. This does not take the place of reading the Word, but it accomplishes additional discipline and training. An additional advantage is that throughout the day, you can continue to work the passage, building your spirit, meditating day and night.

Hebrews 4:12 says, **For the Word of God is living and powerful...** It is energizing! As the revealing of the Word delights your heart and soul, grace floods the soul and the physical body is energized by the life flowing from God's Word. What a heavenly experience—and healthy for your earth suit! **For they are life to those who find them, and health to all their flesh.** (Proverbs 4:22).

An interesting scripture appears in Ephesians 5:26 concerning Christ and the church: **that He might sanctify and cleanse her with the washing of water by the word.** A curious thing happens as the soul is renewed or washed by the Word. Certain impurities start surfacing—impurities in the soul that need to be washed away. That might include ways of thinking that are contrary to heaven's best, old habits that have made deep ruts in the mind, strongholds created by offenses, bitterness, emotional ties or cares of this world. The list goes on. But why make a list? Why actively pursue attempting to identify every wrong way of thinking and doing? When the 'right' shows up, all the wrong will be obvious and go. It is like teaching tellers in the bank how to identify counterfeit money. They don't study all the possible counterfeits. They study the real, then the counterfeit is obvious. Impurities will be obvious. It is not necessary to go searching for them. A similar thing happens in the processing of silver ore. When silver ore is refined through a process that necessitates the application of extreme heat, the impurities or dross will surface. In Proverbs 25:4 we read, **Take away the dross from silver, And it will go to the silversmith *for* jewelry.** In Jeremiah 23:29: **Is My Word not a fire...** During the process of the soul being renewed with spiritual truth, the old impurities may surface such as old ways of thinking, old habits, old vocabulary, old anger spells (called *"fits of carnality"* by some).

Receive this Word engrafted to see dross washed away more quickly and easily in your life:

> **Knowing that Christ, having been raised from the dead, dies no more. Death no longer has dominion over Him. For *the death* that he died, He died to sin once for all; but *the life* that He lives, He**

**lives to God. Likewise you also, reckon yourselves to be dead indeed to sin, but alive to God in Christ Jesus our Lord.
Romans 6:9-11**

Take note of the word *likewise*; just like, in the same way reckon also yourselves *"dead to that."* For instance, perhaps in a pressured moment an outburst of angry words surfaces. Now think about it: that is not the new you. That did not come from the heart of the new creation. It is not the fruit of your new God-given righteous nature. That is the old you, the old creation, an old habit. Plainly stated, that is dross. So what do you do? You take care of it with God and ask forgiveness of your neighbor (if necessary). But to the atmosphere around you and before God and your adversary, the devil, having received forgiveness, proclaim, *"I am the righteousness of God in Christ Jesus. That dross is not me, I am dead to that!"* Then start rejoicing and thanking God that you are delivered from that old nature.

For you to rejoice in faith having received the gift of righteousness allows the Holy Spirit to be magnified and remove that dross. It allows an eternal work to manifest in your heart. As long as you keep *trying* to be righteous and keep *trying* not to be angry—as long as you think that's you, and allow sorrow and grief to overcome your heart, you will never have the victory that comes by faith in what Jesus has done. Sorrow and grief will mix that dross right back down into the silver. Then a little while later, here we go with the same dross again. Allow faith and the Spirit of God to have access to your heart and soul. God is an expert refiner!

Likewise you also, reckon yourselves to be dead indeed to sin... Go back to Romans 6:9-11 and put your name in the appropriate places. *"Knowing that I, having been raised from the dead, die no more. Death no longer has dominion over me. For the death that I died, I died to sin once for all; but the life that I live, I live to God."* Galatians 2:20 says that we are crucified with Christ Jesus. In Ephesians 2:6 we see that God has raised us up together in Christ Jesus. The battle is in the soul. Receive your deliverance from yourself and receive it by faith.

Years ago when I was first learning this, my sons had been picking at each other and really had not responded properly or done what I had asked of them. In a moment of frustration (before I understood about controlling my atmosphere) I released a burst of anger. The whole situation could have been handled a different way. As soon as it happened, I knew I had missed the mark. Quickly I caught up with my soul and took it to God. *"Sorry, God, I missed it there, forgive me. Now, boys, I am sorry—I should not have let that frustration have access to my soul. But now I want you to know, that is not me, I am dead to that."*

This may be a very simplistic example; but you would be amazed at how many mothers stay in condemnation concerning their children. No matter how simple or complex, the principles are still the same—recognition, forgiveness, and application of spiritual law. **Likewise you also, reckon yourselves to be dead to sin...** Rom. 6:11. Is that somewhere in the future, perhaps 'over yonder' in heaven? No, you are dead to that now, crucified in Christ Jesus by faith.

CHAPTER FOUR
Poet the Word

Have you ever heard the expression, *"You are a poet and didn't know it"*? Well you are, you know. In James chapter 1 verse 22 God commands us to be doers of the word and not hearers only. The word translated 'doers' in the Greek is a very interesting word. The Greek word is <u>*poietes*</u> which means a performer, especially a poet. That word is translated 'poets' in the book of Acts chapter 17 and verse 28: **For in him we live and move and have our being as certain also of your own <u>poets</u> have said, 'For we are also his offspring.'** Therefore, to be doers of the word is not only to act on the word, or perform the word, but it is also to *poet* the word. James goes on to say, by the inspiration of the Holy Spirit, in Chapter 1 starting with verse 22:

> **But be ye doers** (performers and poets)
> **of the word and not hearers only,**
> **deceiving yourselves. For if anyone is a**
> **hearer of the word and not a doer, he is**
> **like a man observing his natural face in**
> **a mirror, for he observes himself, goes**
> **away and immediately forgets what kind**

of man he was. But he who looks into the perfect law of liberty and continues in it, and is not a forgetful hearer but a doer (a performer, a poet) **of the work, this one will be blessed in what he does** (his performance or poetry)**. If anyone among you thinks he is religious, and does not bridle his tongue but deceives his own heart, this one's religion is useless.**
James 1:22-26

The mirror is the word of God. If a person looks in the mirror and sees that in Christ Jesus he is the righteousness of God, he is a new creation, he is a son or daughter of God, a joint-heir with Jesus, and that person does not act like it (perform and poet that revelation) he will deceive himself. He will think, *"It's all good."* That is only hope without the change. Renovation of the mind requires repetition and discipline to change a person's outward life. On the inside, the inward person is born again of God having received the substitutionary work of Christ and the regeneration of the Holy Spirit. He is a son or a daughter of God, a new creation, the righteousness of God, and a joint-heir with Jesus. For that to be manifest in the visible realm, the soul must be renewed or renovated by discipline and repetition. A person must be able to act and speak contrary to the feelings of past memories and old ways of doing things.

This is where making poems of the word is very helpful. If there is a particular area in your life that is not lining up to the truth of God's word in the covenant that you have through Christ Jesus, select several verses that pertain to that subject. Joshua 1:8 says to meditate the word day and night. Then listen to your heart. A poem will evolve for you to repeat over and over and over again until the bands contrary to God's Word are loosed and new pathways are established. That will change the way you think. 3 John verse 2 says that you must prosper and be in health as your soul prospers. Go with the word.

Ephesians 5:18-19 says,

> **And do not be drunk with wine, in which is dissipation; but be filled with the spirit, speaking to one another in psalms and hymns and spiritual songs, singing and making melody in your heart to the Lord.**

The King James translation says, **Speaking to yourselves...** In other words, it does not always have to be a song. It can be a poem when the word of Christ dwells in you richly! If you pay attention to your spirit, there is a word, phrase or song that is floating up out of your spirit. It may be the beginning of a poem relating to the renovation of your mind that will allow who you are in Christ Jesus in the inward man to be manifested in the outward man.

The transformation of the mind requires more than just reading the Word of God to manifest in us what Christ has done for us. It takes the transforming power of the Holy Spirit, the Comforter, the Spirit of truth. Hosea

10:12 says:

> **Sow to yourselves in righteousness, reap in mercy; break up the fallow ground: for it is time to seek the Lord till He come and rain righteousness upon you.**

In Mark chapter 4, Jesus reveals to us that the seed is the Word of God. As you are sowing the good seed of God's Word into your heart by confessing the Word, new pathways are being established in the heart and mind. However, it takes the rain of the Holy Spirit to complete the transformation. I liken this process to digging ditches in preparation for the flood of the Spirit to bring life to your labor. 2 Kings chapter 3 relates an historical account of three kings who were stranded in the desert with no water for themselves or their livestock. By the instruction of the prophet Elisha, they filled the valley with ditches in anticipation of a supernatural provision of water according to the Word of the Lord. Once the ditches were completed, they slept. The next morning the ditches were flooded with life-giving water.

Similarly, as you are mediating on God's Word, confessing and working the Word into your soul and heart, you are digging ditches in expectation for the Holy Spirit to flood those new pathways with His Life-giving Anointing, which will bring vision, direction, heavenly strategies, and manifestation. Being a poet and performer of the Word has no small results.

The following are some examples that you can use.

But it is even better to create your own Book of Psalms or poems that are personal to you, that come from your spirit. They don't have to rhyme. Remember , you are after repetition, acting and speaking contrary to feelings day and night, to renovate the mind and allow the new life you have in Christ to blossom.

Drill a poem that is appropriate to the turning of what has tried to hold your brain down. Read 2 Kings 16. Ditches must be dug contrary to feelings for the Holy Spirit to Flood and bring Living Water to that part of your Promise Land (Soul).

I'm a son (daughter) of God
A new creation
The Righteousness of God
A joint-heir with Jesus

I'm a tither
in covenant with Almighty God
The windows of Heaven are open over me
And the devourer is rebuked

I'm a kingdom of God ambassador
Lawful owner of all
He freely gives me all things
And leads me in the way I should go
I have power to get wealth
Grace to be rich
Blessed with no sorrow
I'm redeemed from the curse

The days of my life are 120 years
As my days, so my strength
He satisfies me with long life
Fills my mouth with good things

    This poem is for the harvest on seed sown into your Pastor and the vision and assignment God has ordained for your church from the foundation of the world. The scripture says you communicate (partner) with those who teach you the word and are a partaker of their graces.

Chosen and ordained
Flowing in the gifts
Known in the gates
Changing nations

Listen to whatever word is floating up out of your spirit. And let the poem flow. Be faithful with the poem God gives you. Experience the shift. Bands in the brain are being loosed so that the real (spiritual) you will manifest victory over facts.

Psalm 126:1-20

> **When the Lord brought back the captivity of Zion, We were like those who dream. Then our mouth was filled with laughter, and our tongue with singing.**

CHAPTER FIVE
Air Traffic Controller

A woman came up to me after a service once and was beaming with excitement. She told me she had spent some time in the armed forces and always dreamed of being an air traffic controller. *"Well, now I am one!"* she said.

Discerning what is happening in your atmosphere and controlling it with divinely empowered weapons is a major key to fighting a successful fight of faith. In Ephesians 2:2, the Holy Spirit informs us that there is a *"prince of the power of the air."* This prince is your adversary, the devil. He is a spirit, but he has been cast out of the spirit world, cast down into the darkness of the mental, psychological, emotional soul world. The soul world is very dark without the illumination of the truth of God. **The entrance of Your words gives light...** (Psalm 119:130). Satan's kingdom is referred to as the kingdom of darkness. When the light of God's Word shows up, he will flee.

Years ago we took a family trip to Mammoth Cave National Park. On one of the underground guided tours, the park ranger took us deep down into one of the large caverns that was entirely illuminated by artificial light.

He directed us to be seated and then he switched off the lights. For the first time in our lives we were in total, absolute darkness. After a couple of minutes he asked us to put our hand directly in front of our eyes. *"Can you see anything at all?"* he asked. *"Absolutely nothing,"* came the reply. Then he lit one solitary paper match—one tiny little flickering flame—and the whole cave with everyone in it was revealed. Darkness can never overtake or cast out light; just a tiny bit of illumination will cause total darkness to flee.

The pressure of your soul world may seem intense sometimes; but just a little understanding from the Word of Life will cause mountains of opposition to be as molehills. **...get wisdom, And with all your getting, get understanding** (Proverbs 4:7). Understanding is the key that unlocks the light for the soul world. And when there is light on the scene, the kingdom of darkness flees. **Therefore submit to God. Resist the devil and he will flee from you. Draw near to God and He will draw near to you...** (James 4:7-8). Too many Christians have been trying to do the second part of that verse without doing the first part. To be divinely powerful, our weapons must be of the spirit through the spiritual revelation of God's Word.

When I was homeschooling my children, part of my instruction in teaching them to read was simply to demonstrate the joy of reading. When Clay was five, he could hardly stand it. He wanted to read for himself so much, he would bring me books and even though he could not yet do it by himself, nonetheless he would still follow the words with his eyes. I would teach him how to sound out words and other things that were helpful, but it seemed so hard and such a struggle. It just did not seem like he would ever be able to do it himself. It was so agonizing and so frustrating until one day, something just clicked. Suddenly, it all came together for him. One day it was so hard, such a struggle, so intimidating; then, like a flash, a light bulb came on and he was reading fluently. Now, it seemed like the easiest thing in the world. *"Why, certainly, I can read. Can't everybody? It's so easy. I was borne reading. Never had a struggle in my life."* What had seemed so hard before—when the light came, when understanding put everything together —it was just as natural as eating.

It is the same way with situations that you struggle with in this natural, temporal world. To your mind, it may seem so difficult and intimidating. But when you draw near to God's Word and receive spiritual understanding, darkness will flee and it will seem as though you have always known what to do in this situation and how to do it. The first step to being an effective air traffic controller who overcomes darkness is to seek first the kingdom of God which is the kingdom of light, the kingdom of understanding. Grant me a *"spirit of wisdom and revelation in the knowledge of you that the eyes my understanding will be enlightened"* (a prayer derived from Ephesians. 1:17). Without the understanding, without the light, an air traffic controller cannot see to direct traffic effectively.

The best piece of understanding I can give you to start you off is that not every thought that runs through your mind is your thought. Remember, the *"prince of the power of the air"*? He tries to be an air traffic controller as well, and comes as a deceiver. That's why in 2 Corinthians 10 we are commanded to take every thought captive to the obedience of Jesus Christ. In other words, whatever thoughts call into question or oppose your position in Christ Jesus as well as any thought that turns your attention from His provision and focuses on your inadequacy, TAKE THEM CAPTIVE. Make your thoughts obey what Jesus says about you.

Now, let us reason together. If your enemy who hates you because you are made in God's image breaks into your house with a red suit on, a forked tail and a dangerous looking pitchfork in his hand, you would really have to work at it to be deceived. *"Get out of my house. You have no right here."* But let us say, that same creature is invisible and has only one thing in which it is very accomplished—imitating. It comes into your mental psychological, emotional soul world and begins imitating your feelings, your voice and way of speaking. *"I am just too tired to go to church tonight. I'll just stay home and watch that movie I've been wanting to watch."* Or how about this, *"What if I had a pain in my chest? What would I do about that? Ooh, what is that? Feels a little uncomfortable. I wonder if I should worry about that? Oh no, that was a sharp pain that time! I better go have it checked out. Heart attacks run in my family."*

I have known of a person who had a little episode like that and became so totally convinced that he was having heart problems that even after extensive tests which were negative. Thoughts came: *"I know that the doctor has missed it. I know I've got problems. He must have misread the test. I've got to have medicine for my heart."* He kept talking about it (and guess what?) he ended up with heart problems.

We know that the speech center is the dominant center in the brain. When the speech center is activated and the person starts speaking what he/she is thinking, the body starts to prepare itself to act on and line up to those words. That's why the Word of Life says in Joel 3:10, **...Let the weak say, 'I am strong'.** Even when you feel weak, if you will say *"I am strong"* repeatedly, that command center of the brain will cause the rest of the body to prepare itself to act on those words.

Not every thought is your thought. Evaluate thoughts before you give them voice. Do not say what you feel, say what you want, what you believe, and the feelings will line up. To be an air traffic controller, you must be a custodian of your thought life. Not every thought is your thought. You may not be able to keep the thoughts from coming, but you can take them captive and keep them from trashing up your soul. Do not just fight a defensive war. Ephesians 6 says that the Word of God is a sword. Take those thoughts captive and counter attack with what God says. Get the last say in the matter. It is your life. You have a right to keep your mind and house clean of intruders. Fight the <u>good</u> fight of faith (2 Cor. 10:3-5).

A second bit of information that is necessary is the fact that words determine atmospheres. I know you have had the opportunity to be in the atmosphere of a pity party. Misery loves company, they say. And when one tells a 'woe is me' story of how hard life is, the next takes on the challenge of topping that woeful tale, presumably to make the first feel better. But then there is always another person who has been wanting more sympathy anyway, and perhaps does not mind exaggerating the bitter things that have happened in their life. Words control atmospheres. And what kind of atmosphere do we have here? We have an atmosphere full of grief, oppression, lack and every vile thing. This is not the wisdom that comes from above, as the book of James says.

Imagine coming into a room where two people have just been hammering at each other, full of anger and strife. The people are no longer there but you can still feel tension in the atmosphere. Or perhaps you have been feeling great all day and you enter into that atmosphere and suddenly feel tight, you know not why. That tightness or tension was caused by words, and may not change until something is spoken out to reverse that.

Why is it that you enjoy being around happy people? Their atmosphere feels good. You are enjoying even the air that you are breathing. So, what do you want to do as an air traffic controller? Be a pity party crasher! Shatter that atmosphere with Words of Life. *"It's a good day! I'm not going to bed the same as when I woke up. I'm learning something in this day. I am stronger today than yesterday. Isn't God good!"* That atmosphere of grief, lack, loss will shatter like crystal. Grief cannot hold up against the joy of the Lord. There is liberty in a joyful atmosphere.

You cannot be an effective air traffic controller unless you acknowledge that there is a war going on in the atmospheric envelope of this planet. God's angels are with us and demons are against us. The fight is in the invisible world which is greatly affected by words and atmospheres. Psalm 103:20 says, **Bless the Lord, you His angels, who excel in strength, who do His word, heeding the voice of His word.** God's Words of Life and faith produce an atmosphere of joy, which is an atmosphere in which God and His angels can work. Words of lack, grief, sorrow, discouragement and frustration produce an atmosphere of oppression in which the demonic realm can work. An atmosphere of joy, which is an atmosphere of faith, is a climate expecting to receive from God. An atmosphere of grief is an atmosphere of fear and unbelief, which is a climate that opposes and rejects God's will and purpose—His promises.

1 Peter 1:13 instructs us to **...gird up the loins of your mind.** Remember the caterpillar changing into a butterfly? Make an investment of time to wrap up your mind with evidence from God's word concerning his Will for you. **Your will be done on earth as it is in heaven** (Matthew 6:10). What is God's will for you in heaven? There are promises and evidence in the Word of God that will produce an atmosphere to receive from Him. Meditate by muttering God's word. Speak it into your heart. And when the evidence of God's will is in your heart in abundance, your mouth will speak and you will receive from heaven.

CHAPTER SIX
A Holy Day

"Tonight, before we do anything else, I am going to use you as guinea pigs." A hush fell over the crowd.

"What is she up to now? I don't know if I want to be a part of this or not." Suspicion was rampant.

"Just relax. It's not that bad. I want to illustrate a point. Now pair off and one of you be the patient and the other the doctor—soul doctor that is. OK, soul doctors, instruct your patients to hold their arms level with their shoulders. Now, patients, think of an event in your life that was a disappointment, perhaps it had some sadness with it. Something you really don't like to think about. Okay, doctors, test the strength of their arms. They are very weak, correct? Now, level your arm again and think of the joy of the Lord. Think about heaven; think about the joy of seeing Jesus face to face. He's going to wipe away all tears. There will be no more grief, no sorrow, no death. Glory to God. God is so good. Test the strength of that arm now. See the difference? Grief weakens—joy strengthens."

In Nehemiah Chapter Eight it says:

> "This day is holy to the Lord your God; do not mourn nor weep." For all the people wept, when they heard the words of the Law. Then he said to them, "Go your way, eat the fat, drink the sweet, and send portions to those for whom nothing is prepared; for this day is holy to our Lord. Do not sorrow, for the joy of the Lord is your strength."
> **Nehemiah 8:9-10**

    This is an interesting concept. Many of you may not have considered that grief is <u>not holy</u>. We can see from this passage that an atmosphere of grief is the opposite of a holy atmosphere. Don't get me wrong! Seriously examining your life and opening your heart for correction and instruction are vital to change. But how many times do you have to 'feel' sorry or regret a past sin? If repentance is active, rejoice in your deliverance. Now take the next step: A holy atmosphere is an atmosphere overflowing with the joy of the Lord and full of strength and power.

    In the past, many of us may have understood 'holy' in a very different way. In a holy atmosphere, everyone had to be quiet and still or at least unnoticeable. Smiling and laughing were frowned upon—kneeling and praying would be the correct posture. Oh yes, and do not forget *"examining yourselves"* for sin. Surely you could come up with something you have not confessed. And if there were no sins of commission, surely a sin of omission would surface. After all...**all have sinned and fall short**

of the glory of God (Romans 3:23).

Some of you may be thinking that holy simply means set apart unto God. But what kind of God do we serve? A God who is fault finding and demanding; or a loving father who says, *"I will make all grace abound to you through the gift of faith to give you world overcoming power."* **In Your Presence is fullness of joy** (Psalm 16:11). In His presence is not grief. A holy day set apart unto God is a day full of joy in His Presence. This is not to be confused with worldly joy which is accessed through movies, ball games, parties, etc. When the truth of the word of God is unveiled there is joy in His Presence that surpasses happiness.

Let us imagine the time when Jesus walked this earth in a body of flesh and blood. Jesus was going about healing all who were oppressed by the devil. In a particular place, there was leprosy which was incurable and the people in the leper colony had no hope. They were separated from family and friends and did not know that it was God's will for them to be healed. (Jesus performed the will of the Father in the earth. He said in John 14:9, **He who has seen me has seen the father.**)

Imagine that you are a leper in that colony and you hear of Jesus' ministry—the healing prophet. Many lepers are leaving the colony never to return. You are thinking, *"If he healed all those multitudes, I am no different from them. I know He can heal me. But is He willing? No one ever told me before that it was God's will for me to be healed. But I know this Jesus is sent from God. How else could He do all these miracles?"* So you go on a quest to see Jesus. And when you find

Him you worship Him for all the good you have heard of Him and because of the love and joy that is in His presence. *"Lord, I know if you are willing you can make me whole."* And as He stretches out His hand toward you He says, *"I am willing."* In that instant of time the eyes of your understanding are enlightened. *"It is God's will to heal. I have been deceived all my life."* Your way of thinking is suddenly changed. Joy floods your soul and He says, *"Be healed."*

It is a holy day! God's will is being done in the earth as it is in heaven. It is not a day full of grief and sorrow for sin, but a day filled with the joy of the revealed word of how good God is and how good His provision through Christ Jesus is. Changing your way of thinking about God through revealed truth is true repentance—and it is joyous.

2 Corinthians 5:21 says, **For He made Him who knew no sin to be sin for us, that we might become the righteousness of God in Him.** When you are born again, you are made the righteousness of God. You are a new creation, made in the image of God in your spirit. When your mind is renewed concerning new creation realities, the righteousness of God has expression in the outer man and victory over sin is the result. The righteousness of God cannot sin. Therefore, repentance is more than just confessing sin, it is renewing your mind or changing your way of thinking concerning new creation realities. That allows who you are on the inside to have expression on the outside. Repent! It is a joyous thing! Change your way of thinking so that the 'same old, same old' will no longer dominate your life.

Repentance becomes an attitude more than an event. An attitude of repentance expects and looks for lights to come on in the mind and heart and looks for correction and adjustments every day.

We had a dog, Rusty, who had a temptation in his dog-nature life that was disgusting. I punished him for it, attempted to remove the temptation, and even tried to direct his attention toward something else. He knew he was not supposed to eat that. He knew he would get punished for it. He really hated the consequences of his actions, but did not hate the sin. It was his nature. He was a dog. What was the temptation that was more than he could bear? He thought 'cat poop' was a delicacy. The protein content of cat food is very high and therefore much of it passes on through the cat's system. The dog nature does not consider the source—only the smell and taste. **A man who is in honor, yet does not understand, is like the beasts that perish.** (Psalm 49:20) I have never in all my existence been tempted to eat 'cat poop'. Why? I am not a dog. I do not have a dog nature. When we truly pursue and realize who we are in Christ, the Righteousness of God, a new creature, that the sin nature is dead, and we have a new nature, sin is like 'cat poop'! *"Are you kidding me—Sin? Why would I be interested in 'cat poop'? That's disgusting! It's not my nature. I don't have a sin nature anymore."*

Refuse to go to bed the same as you woke up. Add that confession to your morning routine. If you have done all you know to do, that is good news for the Christian. You just do not know enough. You are going to learn something today. You are willing to hear, be obedient and let the scripture come alive in your heart to give you greater understanding.

...Do not sorrow, for the Joy of the Lord is your strength (Nehemiah 8:10b). How is that strength to be used? Is it merely a release for us to giggle a little and give us some relief from the 'long, burdensome path of life'? That is far from it! Its purpose is to give us God's strength which will allow us to harvest the promises God has for us. It will bring life to dead situations, preserve life, and cast out grief and death. It is a powerful force! 1 Peter 1:6-9 says:

> **In this you greatly rejoice, though now for a little while, if need be, you have been grieved by various trials, that the genuineness of your faith, being much more precious than gold that perishes, though it is tested by fire, may be found to praise, honor, and glory at the revelation of Jesus Christ, whom having not seen you love, Though now you do not see Him, yet believing, you rejoice with joy inexpressible and full of glory, receiving the end of your faith-**
> **the salvation of your souls.**

In verse six you must ask yourself this question: Who is the *"you"* referred to in this passage? Is it you, spirit, or is it you, soul? Remember, you are spirit, born again, a new creation in Christ Jesus and Ephesians 2:6 says that God has **...raised us up together, and made us sit together in the heavenly places in Christ Jesus.** That would be, **Far above all principality and power...** Ephesians 1:21.

By reading James 1:13 we can see that God is not the one doing the tempting. The culprit is your adversary, the devil. We know that the accuser of the brethren has been cast out of heaven (Luke 10:18) and the heavens where God dwells have been cleansed by the blood of Jesus (Hebrews 9:23). Where was he cast down into but that dark mental, psychological feeling realm we call the soul world. The devil is the tempter. He is limited to soulish weapons of deceit—both mental and emotional. So who is the *"you"* in verse six of this passage? It is referring to your soul which is pressured by many things from many directions. The battle is in the soul world.

Look at verse nine again. There is an end to your faith being tried. The end is that your soul is saved or delivered into a higher spiritual reality. **Receive with meekness the implanted word, which is able to save your souls** (James 1:21b). **By your patience possess your souls** (Luke 21:19).

When your mind, emotions, and your will are saved into a higher spiritual reality, the manifestation of what God has promised you is realized. You have read in the Word of God that by the stripes Jesus took on His back you were healed (1 Peter 2:24). The provision for sins being washed away into the sea of forgetfulness was given through Jesus Christ almost two thousand years ago. So was the provision for the healing of your body. The healing you see provided in the Word is realized, individually, when the soul is saved in that area. **Beloved, I pray that you may prosper in all things and be in health, just as your soul prospers** (3 John 2).

What do we mean by a higher spiritual reality? Hebrews 11:3 suggests that everything in this natural realm is created out of the spiritual, unseen realm. In other words, the unseen, spiritual world is more real than what is seen. God is spirit. Jesus is now seated at the right hand of the Father. The promises of God, His provision for your well-being, are spiritual and unseen. Faith is the agent that brings that provision into the seen world and it is accomplished through winning the battle in the soul. When the soul is enabled to escape into the resting place of spiritual reality, when the soul 'sees' something more real than what it has been 'seeing' through natural means, when God's provision is more real to the soul than the natural seen facts, salvation has come and the promise manifests in the seen world.

Go back to verse eight and we see that there is a gift God has given us to harvest this victory. In Galatians 5:22 we see that Joy is a fruit of your spirit. Actually joy is a spiritual force that your soul can tap into which will allow your faith to work more effectively. How will you receive the end of your faith? (A good end, I might add) You receive with Joy unspeakable and full of the glory of God!

Now—back to our example at the beginning of this chapter. Joy strengthens and grief weakens. In First Corinthians 15 we are informed that death is the last enemy to be destroyed. Grief and death go hand in hand. Where you find grief, you find death to the promises of

God. Why? Because grief is an atmosphere of unbelief which is brought on by the adversary to keep you from experiencing God's goodness. Right before a breakthrough is about to happen for your soul, right before the manifestation you are believing for, grief may come to try to weaken your soul and cut off your victory. Well, grief/death is the last enemy to be destroyed. When the attack comes, start rejoicing because you are at the end, the home stretch, the finish line is just ahead. Know that joy is strength and grief is weakness—is it hard to understand that grief cannot sustain an attack against the Joy of the Lord? It is just like drilling for water in a drought. The more pressure the water is under, the stronger it will flow. If pressure is mounting and frustration and confusion are trying to hinder your soul, get up out of your seat, put on some praise the Lord music, and dance. Hit one of those Joy gushers, Victory is sweet. It's a Holy Day.

...Weeping may endure for a night but Joy comes in the morning (Psalm 30:5).

CHAPTER SEVEN
Tourniquets in the Soul

"I think your phone is ringing."

"The phone? Oh yes, you're right. Here it is. Hello?"

Much to my surprise, calling on my cell phone as we were driving home from church in Lexington was my older son, Clay. He was seven hundred miles away at college and had been experiencing some very disquieting symptoms in his physical body. He explained that all day his heart had been fluttering, then skipping beats, and he was 'feeling funny.' Fear was trying to gain entrance to his mind and I could tell he needed help. I immediately diagnosed the problem and began speaking comforting words to him to quiet his mind. I knew that he understood the Word of Life and what Jesus provided through his death and resurrection and that God was on his side. I spoke directly into his spirit concerning the strength and born again righteous life that was in him and his divine destiny that was yet to be fulfilled. Now with his soul quieted and his spirit strengthened, we prayed. *"Lord, we believe by the stripes of Jesus, Clay's body is healthy and whole, his heart is strong. We believe we receive that in Jesus' name."* **...whatever things you ask**

when you pray, believe that you receive them, and you will have them (Mk 11:24). Then I cast out the fear that was trying to gain access. Immediately peace flooded his soul and body and the symptoms left. With his atmosphere controlled and his body feeling better, he was able to receive instruction. In a brief discussion we both could see what had allowed those symptoms to have access to his body. He had taken quite a bit of pressure on his soul and had not continued a strong corresponding rhythm of faith (see Chapter 2).

Jesus said, **In the world you will have tribulation; but be of good cheer, I have overcome the world** (John 16:33). As long as we abide in Him, the vine, and maintain a strong rhythm and relationship with Jesus, the pressure or strength of the spirit can overcome any outside pressure. The battle is in the soul world. When the pressure gradient is not in favor of the spirit, a situation arises that is described in Galatians 5:17. When the flesh wars against the spirit and the spirit against the flesh, we cannot do what we wish. This can happen by not feeding the spirit properly (fast the flesh—not the spirit), not maintaining a healthy conscience or conviction, or by pushing your soul and body beyond the boundary of grace that you have accessed to operate in God's strength for your life.

Lack in any of these areas can give way to a condition I call tourniquets in the soul. Think for a moment what a tourniquet will do. Often when a person gives blood at the blood bank or blood is required for certain tests, the operator will place a tight elastic band around the donor's arm to constrict the flow of blood before inserting a needle in the donor's vein. This is necessary to cause blood to flow into a receptacle instead of returning to the body's circulatory system. Now consider these two scriptures. James 2:26 says that **...the body without the spirit is dead.** In other words, no matter how faithfully a person guards that physical body with good nutrition, exercise, and care, when the spirit leaves, the body dies. The spirit is the only real source of life for the body. Therefore we should give the most care to the spirit. Proverbs 4:23 states, **Keep** (guard) **your heart with all diligence, for out of it spring the issues** (forces) **of life.** Out of the spiritual heart flows the very life force that is necessary for the physical body. Verse 22 of the same chapter also states that the Word is life to those who find them and health (other translations say " 'medicine') to all their flesh. Evidently feeding the spirit Words of Life will be like medicine and produce health in the physical body.

This is an important point. Remember our discussion of the caterpillar and the butterfly? In the analogy our transformation involved the renewing of the mental psychological realm of the soul. It can easily be seen that the soul is the gate between the spirit realm and the physical realm. If there exists pressure or some type of hindrance in the soul realm, the flow of life from the spirit into the flesh is restricted. Whenever the force of life flowing to the flesh body is weakened, that 'earth suit' becomes more susceptible to sickness and disease. Is it any surprise that doctors frequently make a diagnosis of 'stress' when explaining certain symptoms? If the stress or tourniquet in the soul continues, certain unalterable conditions may arise (unalterable, that is, from a natural viewpoint. Praise God for a supernatural God!). And who do you think brings the tourniquet? It is not God. He has the escape. **...this is the victory that has overcome the world—even our faith** (I John 5:4). Jesus says that, **The thief does not come except to steal, and to kill, and to destroy. I have come that they may have life, and that they may have *it* more abundantly** (John 10:10). The thief, the adversary, satan and his crew are in that mental, psychological feeling realm. That is where the battle is and that is the gate through which spirit life must pass to release life into the physical body. Applying your faith to such confessions as, *"I am the righteousness of God in Christ Jesus. I am a new creation. Christ became a curse to redeem me from the curse. By His stripes I was healed. He took my infirmities and bore my sicknesses,"* open the gate for spirit life to flow freely.

Condemnation teaching which emphasizes the inability of the flesh to obey God and constantly focuses on how far short our flesh has fallen from perfection pressures a person into trying to work for their salvation instead of applying faith in what God has accomplished through Jesus Christ. Condemnation, oppression, confusion, and frustration tend to close the gate. The doctrine of righteousness which teaches who you are in Christ Jesus and how to walk in your right standing before God floods the gate with restorative spirit life.

Your adversary, satan, is self-employed. He is a fallen angel that brought condemnation, oppression, lack, poverty, grief, and consequently corruption to this planet by deceiving people with his lies.

Think of it! The first deception in the Garden of Eden was that Adam and Eve had to do something else to be like God (Genesis 3:5). Righteousness is not how much you know or what you do. It is not right living; it is right standing before God. In the beginning they were righteous, made in God's image. As soon as satan convinced them that they were not like God, not righteous, they acted unrighteously, disobeyed God, and became what they were convinced of, that is unrighteous. They were born-again backwards. A major tourniquet was wrapped around the soul world and corruption entered through satan's deception. Now, through Christ Jesus, the reconciliation has come; but the battle for the full redemption is in the soul world. Righteousness teaching looses tourniquets while condemnation tightens them.

Here is the bottom line. What are you going to believe? Are you going to believe what God says about you or what the adversary and temporal circumstances say about you? Do you have more faith in the devil manifesting hell on earth or God manifesting heaven on earth? One of the most frequently quoted verses in the bible is, **Your will be done on earth as it is in heaven** (Matt 6:10). But do we really believe we can have *"days of heaven on earth"*? I have heard people say, *"The last few months have been nothing short of hell on earth."* Some folks have more faith in the devil's power to bring hell to earth than God's power and provision to bring heaven to earth. Your faith is the deciding factor. How will you choose to use your time today? Will you apply yourself to learn the ways and language of the kingdom of heaven or will you let another day go by while you float downstream with all the rest? Any dead fish can float downstream. Why not do something that will make an eternal difference in your life and the lives of others today. One of satan's favorite tourniquets to oppress the soul is lack, especially financial lack. Choose to learn how to let the life of God flow in your life and defeat the plans of the enemy.

CHAPTER EIGHT
The Covenant Bridge

In the beginning God created the heavens and the earth. The earth was without form, and void; and darkness *was* on the face of the deep. And the Spirit of God was hovering over the face of the deep. And God said, "Let there be light"; and there was light. (or, Light be; and light was)
And God saw the light, that *it was* good.
       Genesis 1:1-4

 God wanted a family—sons and daughters like Himself—who could think like Him, see and hear like He sees and hears, Love like He loves and communicate with Him. He was creating a place for them to live that was exactly like what He had. He took of the seeds of heaven and planted a garden in the earth. It was perfect in every way, beautifully situated for His family.

Then God saw everything that He had made, and indeed *it was* very good...
       Genesis 1:31a

Then God said, "Let Us make man in Our image, according to our likeness; let them have dominion…over all the earth…" So God created man in His *own* image, in the image of God He created him; male and female He created them. Then God blessed them, and God said to them, "Be fruitful, multiply; fill the earth and subdue it; have dominion…
                              Genesis 1:26-28

Then the Lord God took the man and put him in the Garden of Eden to tend and keep it.   Genesis 2:15

It was a beautiful garden and every tree was pleasant to the sight and good for food. There were rivers and beautiful stones, gold and every perfect thing a person could imagine, and more. There was no corruption, no strife. The animals were beautiful and friendly, no killing, lack or anger. It was a heaven on earth environment with the Blessing of the Lord empowering every breath. What more could God have done to create a perfect environment for His family? Whatever a person could desire was already provided. What more could He have said? What more could He have provided? Man was made to be just like God in every aspect, except for one important exception: God was the Creator, man the creation. God was the source of all Life and Blessing. Man being the creation was totally dependent on the Source for life, health, increase and fulfillment of their

God-given destiny and assignment in this earth realm.

God had given man dominion over the earth. He had provided for his every desire, given him an assignment to take of the seed of the Garden and fill the earth with heaven's provision. Then God empowered him with the Blessing of the Lord to fulfill his destiny: **be fruitful, multiply, fill the earth, and subdue it.** However, because God had given man dominion over the earth, even though the earth is the Lord's and the fulness thereof, He no longer had dominion.

God is sovereign. He does whatever He desires. His will is sovereign. Once He had released His word which was according to His Will, He never changes. It was God's will to give His dominion to His son, Adam. But God was still the Source of Life. Maintaining the Blessing and Life flow in the Garden required God's continual influence. God required a channel through which He could continue to uphold His creation. To ensure man's total victory and success, God instituted the guarantee that would allow God to walk with man, impart wisdom and understanding, replenish, maintain and increase the flow of Life, Strength and the Blessing. He provided covenant for Adam.

We see this connection established by God in verse 16 and 17 of Genesis chapter 2:

> **And the Lord God commanded the man, saying, "Of every tree of the garden you may freely eat; but of the tree of the knowledge of good and evil, you shall not eat, for in the day that you**

eat of it you shall surely die."

This is what we call the covenant bridge which defines our covenant partnership with God. God had given His man total dominion on the earth and the responsibility to order it. If a man did not do it, nothing could be done. In order to fulfill God's dream for the earth He needed someone in a physical body who would obey Him and act in covenant toward Him. In order for Adam to do what he was created to do, he needed God's omnipotence, omniscience and His omnipresence.

The number one rule of covenant is to give the covenant partner your first and your best. This action of faith provides a bridge whereby provision from heaven and the source of life can empower the life and growth on earth. As long as this bridge is strong and active, success on earth is assured for any man who speaks God's words after Him. It all depends on walking with God, hearing the voice of the Good Shepherd, seeing like He sees, and speaking like He speaks.

Jesus modeled this covenant authority. He said that He only spoke what He heard His Father say and only did what He saw His Father do. **...The words that I speak to you I do not speak on My own authority; but the Father who dwells in Me does the works.** (John 14:10) And, **I can of Myself do nothing. As I hear, I judge...** (John 5:30)

Understand the covenant provision for complete victory and success! If Adam would cherish this tree, to dress it and keep it, honoring the fruit as holy belonging to their Source of Life, Love, and Blessing, if they did not eat of it, they would **surely** live, increase and walk with God. **The tree of the knowledge of good and evil was not Adam and Eve's downfall. It was their guarantee for success.**

Since God had given Adam dominion over the earth, He could not come and take His fruit from the tree Himself. Adam would be in charge of something that belonged to God and care for it and gather it for Him. He would bring it to God and God would walk with him and empower him with heaven's best wisdom and strength. As soon as Adam and Eve broke covenant with God by believing the words of the defeated, deceiving devil instead of the Words of God, the Blessing was cut off and the curse devoured the earth.

When the covenant was broken, the pathway for the Blessing was cut off. The curse of sin, sickness, poverty and death was released on the earth. Just as darkness is simply an absence of light, the curse is the absence of the Blessing. But the fall of man did not stop the Father's dream. Even when God's chosen people, led by Moses, refused to obey God, act in covenant, and step into the Promised Land (see Numbers 13-14), God responded to Moses' intercession for the people: **Truly, as I live, all the earth shall be filled with the Glory of the Lord!** (Numbers 14:21) The expression of this principle in the New Testament is: **If we are faithless, He remains faithful; He cannot deny Himself.** (2 Timothy 2:13)

The testimony of Cain and Abel is a beautiful example of God's faithfulness:

And in the process of time (Hebrew: at the

> end of days) **it came to pass that Cain brought an offering of the fruit of the ground to the Lord. Abel also brought of the first born of his flock and of their fat. And the Lord respected Abel and his offering, but He did not respect Cain and his offering. And Cain was very angry, and his countenance fell. So the Lord said to Cain, "Why are you angry? And why has your countenance fallen? If you do well, will you not be accepted? And if you do not do well, sin lies at the door..."**
> **Genesis 4:3-7**

Even though Adam had broken covenant with God and let the curse of sin, lack, and death dominate the earth, Abel discovered a way to build a covenant bridge that would allow God's 'super' to be evident on Abel's 'natural'! Even though it looked as though all was lost, Abel remembered God's promise that the seed of the woman would bruise the head of the serpent. (Genesis 3:15) God had a plan of redemption. Abel acted on that Word and as a covenant action he gave the first and the best to God as an offering. Because of that, God was able to Bless Abel's flocks and all that he had. And He did. It was obvious that the Blessing of the Lord was with Abel. Cain became jealous of his brother's prosperity.

God's warning to Cain is very interesting. *"If you do well"*—act in covenant, bring the first and the best, and build a covenant bridge for the Blessing to flow—*"will you not be accepted?"* You will prosper just as Able has prospered supernaturally. If you do not, the curse of sin will overtake you. Walking in covenant with God has an additional benefit: there is power to overcome sin.

Now let us take a look at Abraham, the Father of Faith. Jesus Christ came to redeem us from the curse according to Galatians 3:13-14, so that the Blessing of Abraham might come on us. What a price Jesus paid for our redemption! How important is it for us to understand that Blessing and walk in it which allows Jesus Christ to be Glorified in our supernatural lifestyle?!

In Genesis 14:18-20 Melchizedek, priest of the Most High God, brought the elements of a covenant meal to Abraham in order to release the Blessing on his life because of Abraham's obedience and faith in God.

> **And he blessed him, and said, "Blessed be Abram of God Most High, possessor of heaven and earth; and blessed be God Most High, who has delivered your enemies into your hand." And he** (Abram) **gave him** (Melchizedek) **a tithe** (the first and best) **of all.**
> **Gen. 14:18-20**

The same supernatural empowerment to prosper that was released on Adam, which he waved off by breaking covenant with God, the same supernatural empowerment with which Abel connected, is now being released on Abram through God's representative! And what is

Abram's response? He immediately responded in covenant to connect with that Blessing through the covenant bridge, the first and best, the tithe. After this covenant, Abram was so confident of the Blessing and his covenant bridge, the tithe, that he responded to the King of Sodom's offer of the spoils of the battle:

> **But Abram said to the King of Sodom,**
> **"I have raised my hand** (a covenant witness) **to the Lord, God Most High,**
> **the Possessor of heaven and earth,**
> **that I will *take* nothing from a thread to**
> **a sandal strap, and that I will not take**
> **anything that is yours, lest you should**
> **say, 'I have made Abram rich...**
> **Gen. 14:22-23**

In other words, *"No one but God will ever be credited with making Abram rich."* Abraham was not only extremely wealthy, but he had a son when he was one hundred years old and his wife was ninety years of age. He was a tither, giving God the first and the best, which was his tree of the knowledge of good and evil.

Let us follow the witness of Melchizedek and Abraham in the New Testament. In the book of Hebrews we find Messianic Jews (Jewish believers in Christ) who are being tempted to go back to temple worship under the Levitical priesthood and animal sacrifices. It certainly is understandable, for this is how they were raised, even though now they have found forgiveness of sins and the eternal Passover Lamb in Jesus the Messiah.

In chapter seven of Hebrews, the writer of Hebrews is bringing the Melchizedek/Abraham incident into focus in order to show how much better the order of Melchizedek is than the Levitical order of Aaron under the Mosaic Law. Since Levi (the Father of the Levitical priesthood) was a descendent of Abraham, and Abraham paid the tenth to Melchizedek, then **...beyond all contradiction the lesser is blessed by the better.** (Hebrews 7:7) Since Melchizedek blessed Abraham, we know that the Levitical priesthood which flowed out of Abraham is the 'lesser.' The Jewish Christians had been in the habit of taking their tithes to the Jewish temple; but now they should take them to Jesus and His Church. **Here mortal men receive tithes, but there He *receives them*, of whom it is witnessed that He lives.** (Hebrews 7:8) In the context of this passage, the writer is referring to the order of Melchizedek. However, we read in verse seventeen of this same chapter, God testifies of Jesus: **...You are a priest forever according the order of Melchizedek.** (Hebrews 7:17) The inference that Jesus should receive our tithes through His Body, the church, is not out of order: *"He lives!"*

Jesus came and became sin that we might become the righteousness of God in Christ Jesus. He redeemed us from the curse (review Deuteronomy 28:15-68) having been made a curse for us. He restored everything that was lost in Adam's transgression. Now He has been set at the right hand of the Majesty in the heavens. Man still has dominion over the earth. The 'lease' is not up yet. We have a second chance. We can access that blessing through the tithe, the first and the best. It is a covenant bridge which allows the Life and Blessing of the Lord to flow supernaturally. If we have received Jesus as our Lord and Savior and eat the tithe, Malachi 3 says that we are robbing from God. Just as the fruit of the tree of knowledge of good and evil did not belong to Adam, God has ordained that the tenth is holy. It belongs to Him. With our obedience, with God's wisdom, power and partnership, we can have the Garden of Eden in our lives again.

CHAPTER NINE
Guard the Garden

Let's go back to the first three chapters of Genesis, back to the Garden of Eden and get the big picture. When God created the heavens and the earth He said that it was very good. There was no grief or sorrow, no corruption, no poverty, no sickness and disease. The world was full of the God kind of life. Wellsprings of joy flooded the creation. There was life and that more abundantly. Fountains of joy flowed out of the hearts of God's people and kept the corrupting influence of grief from having any expression at all. Adam and Eve were clothed in the Glory of Almighty God. And in His presence and in His Glory is fullness of joy (Psalm 16:11)! They were made in the image of God and like God, righteous within and holy without.

But then the tempter entered in...full of questions, confusion, and doubt. As you study that passage in Genesis chapter 3 you will find that the temptation was to forget their image or their god-likeness. **...you will be** (future tense) **like God...**Genesis 3:5. They already were as God, made in His image, god-like, righteous. As soon as they ate of the fruit of the tree of the knowledge of good and evil, they were applying their faith to the devil's lie—that they were not righteous—and they received unrighteous standing before God. Since they chose to believe that they were unrighteous and transgressed covenant, their righteous robes of Glory left them. Faith in God's provision of righteousness was no longer present to manifest heaven (God's glory) on earth. They were born again backwards. Their souls fell into a realm of darkness, which is carnal-mindedness.

When Adam and Eve were first created, the fruit, or outflow, of their spirit was love, peace, faith and joy. But after the fall, grief and fear were in their hearts. In Genesis 2:15, God put Adam in the garden *"to tend and keep it."* The word 'keep' in the Hebrew could be translated 'guard.' He was to guard the garden. But how was Adam to guard it and what would be the effect of his duties? The garden was 'very good' with no corruption, no grief, no sorrow, no sickness or disease, no poverty and no sin. It was, in fact, heaven on earth. And this was also the condition of Adam's heart. There was no grief or sorrow, no sin, sickness or disease, and no lack. Joy overflowed out of his heart like gushers of living water. He was made in the image and likeness of God and his words were full of life. Proverbs 18:21 says, **Death and life *are* in the power of the tongue...** But there was no death in Adam's words, just life. He had the power of life in his words. Jesus Himself said, **...The words that I speak to you are spirit, and *they* are life.** (John 6:63)

Jesus was called the last Adam. What does Proverbs 4:23 state? **Keep your heart with all diligence, for out of it *spring* the issues** (or forces) **of life.** God's will was for Adam to keep life, maintain life, and guard the life of His creation by guarding his heart. Letting the life-giving force of joy flow as living water out of his heart would keep the garden free of grief, corruption, and lack. As long as he kept his heart, he would keep the garden. When he chose to listen to and obey the words of the adversary, he conceived those words of unbelief and fear in his heart. Because he believed the devil and acted on his words, satan became his lord and **...the god of this world...** 2 Corinthians 4:4 (KJV).

Since the fruit of his spirit was no longer joy and love, but instead grief and fear, the creation (including Adam's physical body) became subject to corruption. The power of words is displayed in this passage from Psalm 109:18: **As he clothed himself with cursing as with his garment, so let it enter his body like water, and like oil into his bones.**

It is interesting that a good percentage of the immune system is produced in the marrow of the bones. Words have an effect on the immune system just as surely as grief has an effect on your physical strength (See Chapter 5). The Biblical definition of cursing is not just speaking socially unacceptable words to express oneself in a vulgar way. Deuteronomy 28:15-68 lists the curses, plagues, lack, grief, and repudiations of humanity that have access to this world when people listen to and obey the devil's words. Receiving those words and speaking in agreement with lack, loss, grief, and fear are curse words according to the Bible. Common, worldly vernacular such as, *"That scared me to death,"* or, *"Just the thought of it made me sick,"* was not in the Garden.

Those phrases developed as soon as the curse—grief, fear and corruption—were loosed on the planet.

Many scriptures in the Word of God link grief and dimness of eyesight together. In Genesis 26:35 we read that Esau's wives were a *"grief of mind"* to Isaac and Rebecca. The next verse comments that Isaac was old and his eyes were dim. He called Esau to him to bestow his blessing upon him because he thought he was dying. Yet he lived another twenty years! Psalm 6:7 reads, **My eye wastes away because of grief; It grows old because of all my enemies.** And in Psalm 31:9: **Have mercy upon me, O Lord, for I am in trouble; my eye wastes away with grief...** Watch Psalm 119:123: **My eyes fail** *from seeking* **Your salvation and Your righteous word.** In other words, salvation and the gift of righteousness should bring light, healing, and restoration to the eyes! Now, look at Deuteronomy 34:7: **Moses was one hundred and twenty years old when he died. His eyes were not dim nor his natural vigor diminished.** Moses' atmosphere must have been free of grief and full of joy. He spent a lot of time in the Presence of God where there is fullness of joy, heaven on earth. Moses must have been full of joy; and it had an effect on his physical body. Moses wrote several songs recorded in the Word of God. He must not have had 'curse words' in his vocabulary.

Let's go back to 'garden language' and have garden results! Practice abiding in the Presence of God and worshiping Him for His goodness. It's healthy! If you have received Jesus as your Savior and confess Him as Lord of your life, you are born again, born of God.

Galatians 5:22 states that the fruit of the born of God spirit is love, joy, peace, faith, etc. That is the real you. 2Timothy 1:7 says, **For God has not given us a spirit of fear, but of power and of love and of a sound mind.** In your spirit there are potential gushers of love, joy, and faith that can be tapped into at any time.

When my boys were home from college during their fall break, we went to Pine Mountain State Park for an overnight trip. As we were hiking trails, the boys started playing and joking with each other on the edge of cliffs with big drop offs. Needless to say, my 'soul' was beginning to feel some pressure in the atmosphere from fear. I recognized that fear was not being produced by my born-again spirit. Galatians 5:23 says faith is the fruit of my spirit, not fear. Fear is the opposite of faith. So, instead of giving way and giving place to fear in my soul, I began speaking the Word of God to counter that atmosphere. *"I've not been given a spirit of fear, but power, love, and a sound mind."* (2 Timothy 1:7). *"He that dwells in the secret place of the most high shall abide under the shadow of the Almighty. No evil can befall us, no plague come nigh this dwelling. He has given His angels charge over us to guard us in all of our ways"* (Psalm 91). Then up out of my spirit came this response, *"No evil befalls the righteous"* (Proverbs 12:21). Suddenly, the peace of God flooded my heart and soul. There was no more fear anywhere. The atmosphere was clear. I said nothing to the boys and pretty soon they stopped playing on the edge of the cliff and went on.

When contrary winds are affecting your 'soular'

(radar) atmospheric equipment, start speaking the Word of God, even if you must simply read it out loud directly from the Book. You are drilling for gushers that will save your soul from loss and destruction. John 10:10 states that the thief comes to steal, kill, and destroy. Contrary atmospheres will cut off the life flow from your spirit. In I Peter we read about joy gushers that will produce the same salvation.

> **Whom having not seen you love. Though now you do not see *Him*, yet believing, you rejoice with joy inexpressible and full of glory, receiving the end of your faith— the salvation of your souls.**
> **1 Peter 1:8-9**

When your soul is saved into greater spiritual reality, then 'garden living' or the reconciliation that Jesus Christ provided for you in His death, burial and resurrection are available here and now. **Your kingdom come. Your will be done...** Matthew 6:10.

'Garden living' is not only possible, it pleases God. Jesus Christ has made it possible through His completed work. Having received His work in our hearts, we have only contrary atmospheres with which to deal. The forces of life in your spirit can break through those atmospheres and manifest God's goodness in the earth. The gate is the mind of the soul. **...be transformed by the renewing of your mind...** (Romans 12:2). **Beloved, I pray that you may prosper in all things and be in health, just as your soul prospers** (3 John 2).

CHAPTER TEN
Oxymoron

An oxymoron is a figure of speech in which opposite or contradictory ideas or terms are combined. That is, two or three words which are used together but have opposite or contradictory meaning. For example, jumbo shrimp is an oxymoron. In Romeo and Juliet, he says, *"Parting is such sweet sorrow."* Some other examples would be: pretty ugly, awful pretty, and serious laughter. Actually the word itself is an oxymoron. *'Oxy'* means sharp and *'moron'* means dull. An oxymoron is a phrase that is sharply dull.

This is the oxymoron we will be discussing in this chapter: tribulating saints. *"You must go through tribulation, brother."* *"When God brings you out of Egypt, He takes you into the wilderness."* *"There is always a wilderness on the way to the Promised Land."* *"God must humble you, so He can bless you."* *"Just grin and bear it and give the good Lord the glory."* That describes a tribulating saint. A tribulating saint will be talking more about the battle than the victory.

Have you ever encountered a pity party? A pity party is a party where there is a contest going on—whoever tells the most pitiful story and receives the most sympathy wins (or looses). One might start with how long it took to get to work today and how much trouble they encountered. The next will respond with, *"You think that is something, well how about this..."* And the third just shakes their head and woefully states, *"Oh honey, you just don't know. No one has seen the trouble I've had!"* What is the atmosphere like? A heavy oppression hovers over that party.

Then the next group are Christians. Only these are 'tribulating' Christians. *"Well, you are just lucky to have me at church today." "The devil did this and the devil did that." "The devil has really been after me." "There must really be something big that God has planned for my life because the devil has been fighting me so hard."* In this group, everyone is competing to see who has the most devils occupied. It almost sounds as if the devil is omnipresent. He is not omnipresent. As a matter of fact, when God asked him in the book of Job chapter one where he had been, the answer was *"walking"*. He is walking! If you have all the devils at your house, praise God, someone else is getting some relief. The devil is getting too much praise.

But, Elizabeth, did not Jesus say that in the world you would have tribulation? Yes, but He also said **...be of good cheer, I have overcome the world** (John 16:33). 1 John 4:4 says **...He who is in you is greater than he who is in the world.** He also says in Ephesians 2:6 that He has raised you up and seated you in heavenly places in Christ Jesus. And Ephesians 1:21 says heavenly places are, **Far above all principality, and power, and might, and dominion, and every name that is**

named... Now the question is: Are you a spirit that has a soul; or a little soul creature that has a spirit? If you feel like you are up one day and down the next, that 'yo-yo' is not the real you. You are spirit. That 'yo-yo' is your soul which you are allowing to be thrown about by every wind (or spirit) that comes along. You are responsible to protect and keep your soul from harm. In Isaiah 27:3, the Lord speaks of how He keeps His vineyard. He says **...I water it every moment; lest any hurt it, I keep it night and day.** Wash your soul with the water of the Word and speak to your soul. **Return to your rest, O my soul, for the Lord has dealt bountifully with you.** (Psalms 116:7)

The mental, psychological realm is where the battle is. Your emotions are not to dominate you. Use them as 'soular' equipment to give you information about the atmosphere and your adversary's position. Your 'soular' equipment can pick up on fear that's in the atmosphere. Fear can attach itself to thought patterns or information gathered by your five physical senses. That fear is not you—it is coming at you. **For you did not receive the spirit of bondage again to fear, but you received the Spirit of adoption by whom we cry out, "Abba, Father."** (Romans 8:15)

Before you were born again and became alive to God, your spirit produced fear, but now your spirit produces faith. Fear may feel like it is in you because it is being detected by your emotions, your 'soular' equipment. No matter what the circumstances, you must defeat this atmosphere. John 10:10 says, **The thief does not come except to steal, and to kill and to destroy...** Fear can steal from you and cause you to make wrong or hasty decisions. It can shorten your life span. Treat grief the same way. Have you ever heard of people being sick with grief? The medical profession may tell you these things cannot have any effect on your physical body. Medical school has very limited information on soul sickness. You probably would not ask a car mechanic about nuclear physics. Why ask a doctor of physical medicine about the soul and spirit.

One time in particular I can remember the pressure around me and in the atmosphere being so great that I could not even remember one scripture to bring against it. So, I picked up my Bible and started reading Psalm 119 out loud—louder than the pressuring thoughts of my mind. Fear, grief, failure, you name it, was haunting me. Through teary eyes I kept on reading the Word into the atmosphere until, finally, it shattered just like crystal. That oppressive atmosphere shattered! Suddenly, there was no more fear, grief, or confusion. I felt good and could think straight again. I had won the battle.

Do you see how much of the so called 'wilderness trials' through which people suffer can be ended if they just knew where the battle was? They certainly do not come from your loving heavenly Father. **My people are destroyed for a lack of knowledge...**(Hosea 4:6) The converse of that statement is that with an abundance of the application of the knowledge of God, destruction is cut off. A saint who is always talking about going through tribulation is submitting themselves to much unnecessary 'soulish' trauma. In Psalm 23, the Word says we pass through the valley. Don't camp out there!

Let us return to our discussion of the 'fight of faith.' I am assuming that you know how to feed your spirit, the real you, and you have disciplined your soul with a strong rhythm of faith (see Chapter 2). I want you to think of that rhythm for your soul (such as soul exercises) as practice and preparation for the real race. Let us say you have been reading the Word, doing your confessions, worshiping God and you are strong in your spirit, ready for the day. You leave the house and go about your 'to do' list and suddenly your 'soular equipment' goes off: unexpected bills, symptoms in your body, feelings of failure or loss, fear because of a news report. Then thoughts pass through your mind, *"I had better quit what I'm doing and go home. I must not have prayed right. What have I done wrong? I can never do anything right."* Now, this is the real battle! This is not when you run away and hide or let your 'soular' equipment dominate you. Use it to inform you of the enemy's position and loose those torpedoes of the Word of God that you have been storing up. There is promotion after you have won this battle.

Think of yourself as a Navy Seal—the special forces of the Navy. You have finished your training. You have practiced every possible enemy encounter. You have studied the manual and know how to succeed. Now you are finally out in a submarine on a mission. Suddenly, the radar equipment goes off signaling an enemy approach—lack, loss, grief, fear. Do the Seals scream, get all upset, and turn tail for home? No, this is the moment for which they have been training! Now it is the time for action. A numbness comes over them; they are focused and have concentrated soul control. Then just when the enemy is ready to fire it's best shot—torpedo one: ***By His stripes I was healed***—torpedo two: ***He bore my infirmities, carried my diseases***—torpedo three: ***I am redeemed from the curse of the law***—torpedo four: ***I have authority over all the power of the enemy. Nothing shall by any means hurt me.*** Where is the enemy? He is blasted out of the water.

I was a track and field coach at the college level in the seventies before women's athletics was very advanced. I had several girls who had never done anything athletic. I was not an easy coach. I could see the potential in each person and I wanted that potential to have full expression. We practiced every day for at least two hours. Then would come the big day—the real race. *"Okay girls, you have practiced, you have not missed a day. Now is the time. This is what we've been practicing for. Go get 'em!"* To my amazement, some would come to me scared, complaining about various symptoms and would want to scratch the race (back out at the last minute.) When your 'soular' equipment goes off, don't scratch the race! The race, the battle, is in an unseen realm. When you win over grief, lack, loss, fear, or any other contrary atmosphere with the Word of God and the praises of God, something good is at the finish line for you.

Here is the bottom line. When Adam bowed his knee to a fallen angel by obeying his words, he made satan his lord and therefore, as 2 Corinthians 4:4 states, the *"god of this world."* When Jesus, who knew no sin, became sin for us, He took that nature on Himself through obedience and nailed it to the cross. Through His resurrection He made available to us His righteous nature. He reversed the curse which came as a result of Adam's sin.

Upon receiving Jesus into your heart and making Him Lord of your life, you were born again of God and made a new creation in your spirit—a totally new person, the righteousness of God in Him. But something else happened in that series of events at the cross and resurrection: Jesus ascended to the Father and cleansed the spirit realm of all accusing, condemning demonic activity. No longer can satan approach the throne of God as he did in Job chapter one with his accusations. Hebrew 9:22-24 explains that by the law almost all things are purged with blood, that the heavenly things themselves were purged with better sacrifices than the animal sacrifices. Christ did just that, entering into heaven itself. **Having disarmed principalities and powers, He made a public spectacle of them, triumphing over them in it.** (Colossians 2:15)

The spirit realm is a finished work. What remains is for us to enforce His victory in the mental, psychological, emotional realm so that the victory that Jesus won for us can be made visible in this natural realm. Remember, Ephesians 2:2 calls our adversary the *"prince of the power of the air."* Hebrews 10:13 says Jesus is **...waiting till His enemies are made His footstool.** 1 Corinthians 15:26 states that **...the last enemy that will be destroyed is death.** We still have some work to do. **For the weapons of our warfare are not carnal but mighty in God...** (2 Corinthians 10:4)

The point is this: You are a born again spirit. The enemy is confined to the soul realm. You have the Word of God which is the sword of the spirit (Ephesians 6:17) and He has given you His righteousness. The only weapon satan has is deception. If you have never tried this before, stand in front of a mirror and repeat five times, *"I am the righteousness of God in Christ Jesus."* And believe it. There is power in your tongue. You just released the power of God's Word into the atmosphere. Practice that every day. (If symptoms of oppression persist, triple the dosage.)

Jesus asked us to pray in Matthew 6:10: **Your will be done on earth as it is in heaven.** For God's will to be done on earth as it is in heaven, the deceiver must be overcome. It does not matter what you feel like, it does not matter how it looks. God's Word can fix any problem if you can shake loose the principality that is exalting itself in the soul through deceptions like, *"You don't deserve to be healed. You caused it yourself."* No one deserves to be the righteousness of God. We receive it by faith. Knowing that and confessing it breaks down resistance in the gate between the spirit realm and the natural realm and looses those tourniquets.

In Romans 5:3 we read: **And not only that, but we also Glory in tribulations, knowing that tribulation produces perseverance.** One of the ways you can tell you have released your faith is when tribulation or opposite pressure with its confirming atmospheres and feelings shows up.

Consider this: you are releasing your faith, believing you have received something that belongs to you in

Christ but has been held captive by the deceptions of the enemy. When you release the force of faith, faith grabs the objective and, *"All hell breaks loose!"* Well, it has to break loose for you to manifest what God did for you in Jesus. When the defeated devil breaks loose, he flutters around in your atmosphere for a while full of fear, grief, and lack. ...So who is the 'tribulator'? Who is causing the tribulation? You are! You are 'tribulating' the enemy and then picking up on the effect of it with your 'soular equipment' (emotions). You are disrupting the kingdom of darkness with the light of God's Word. So, rejoice when you encounter disturbances in the atmosphere. You have located the enemy's position. It's time to use your torpedoes and have a heavenly atmosphere with heavenly results.

See it this way. You have been spending time in God's Word. You have been confessing your righteousness and worshiping God. You are praying for others and filling your spirit with a heavenly atmosphere. Words create atmosphere. Since you have been speaking God's Word you have a high-pressure area around you. Now what happens when you encounter a pity party? (In case you are unsure, a pity party would promote a low-pressure area.) Think about the weather. When a high-pressure area encounters a low-pressure area, what do you have—tribulation, a real storm. And who caused that storm? Surely not little, innocent you! As far as your adversary is concerned, you are the offending party. Be a pity party crasher. *"We're having a good day today. Something good is happening in this day. Jesus is alive. We're not going to bed the same as when we woke up."*

There may be a little shaking in the atmosphere but the breakthrough is happening. I have been confronted by situations such as these and responded as I recommended. People witness the lifting of headaches and other pressures. Symptoms of sickness leave in the presence of an atmosphere filled with the Word of God.

Look at what it says in 1 Peter:

> **5 Who are kept by the power of God through faith for salvation ready to be revealed in the last time.**
> **6 In this you greatly rejoice, though now for a little while, if need be, you have been grieved by various trials.**
> **7 That the genuineness of your faith, being much more precious than gold that perishes, though it is tested by fire, may be found to praise, honor, and glory at the revelation of Jesus Christ,**
> **8 whom having not seen you love. Though now you do not see Him, yet believing, you rejoice with joy inexpressible and full of glory,**
> **9 receiving the end of our faith—the salvation of your souls.**
> **I Peter 1:5-9**

That last verse is very interesting. The end of your faith is the salvation of your souls, not a physical manifestation from God. You might think that if a person were being attacked with flu symptoms and they took a stand on the healing provision of Jesus Christ *("He took my infirmities, bore my sicknesses and by His stripes I was healed")*, the end of their faith would be that the symptoms were gone. Yet this verse implies a different understanding. The target of the work of faith should be the soul. Then soul salvation will allow a physical manifestation.

I remember one time in particular my body was experiencing a headache and tiredness, a drained feeling. I was doing my best to fight it off with healing scriptures. *"By His stripes I was healed. If I was healed, I am healed. No weapons formed against me can prosper."* After a while something happened on the inside of me. I'm not talking about the inside of me physically. I'm speaking beyond physical. A break-through, a knowing, a change in attitude manifested. I just sat down on the couch and began to laugh. All the symptoms were still present; but, I knew the fight was over. It was bed time, so I simply went to bed; and, by morning every symptom was gone. The soul had been 'saved' into a higher spiritual reality. The body caught up later.

In another incident with similar symptoms something remarkable occurred. We had made a withdrawal from our heavenly bank account for a trip. We believed we received according to Mark 11:24. When it came time for the trip, we used some other money that we had. However, we knew that particular amount had not yet manifested. Faith has no 'deadlines' so even on the trip and back, we were still thanking God for it. Then those physical symptoms came. Even though I didn't 'feel like' going to church, I still went. (When you make it the law of your life that you will never miss church even if someone must carry you in, something good will happen. **Do not forsake the assembling of yourselves.** Heb 10:25. A corporate anointing can bring a revelation, deliverance, and/or manifestation that a personal anointing at home cannot do.)

As we were leaving church, it 'seemed like' nothing had happened. Symptoms were still heavy on my body. Then someone stopped me as I was getting into the car. They put a check into my hand. As soon as that check hit my hand, I knew the amount without looking at it. As soon as that knowing manifested on the inside, every symptom departed. It was as if a heavy, symptom filled wet blanket had been lifted off my body. Sickness is not just physical. It is a battle that is not flesh and blood but is in the soul world.

Now let's look at 1 Peter one, verse six. Examine the phrase, *"you have been grieved by various trials."* Now the question is: <u>you who</u>? Is the Holy Spirit referring to you, spirit, or you, soul? Peter was writing to a people of like precious faith. In other words, these are people who had been born again of the <u>incorruptible</u> seed of God's Word as he affirms in 1 Peter 1:23. They are created in righteousness and true holiness, new creations, seated in heavenly places in Christ Jesus far above all principalities and powers. And what about the temptations? Who brings temptations? In James 1:13 the scripture reads, **Let no one say when he is tempted, "I am tempted by God"; for God cannot be tempted by evil, nor does He Himself tempt anyone.** God is not the author of the heaviness through manifold temptations.

A study of the scripture will reveal that the tempter is satan (1 Thessalonians 3:15). Since the devil is confined to that mental, psychological realm of the soul, we conclude that the heaviness is in the soul. Even though these people are born again, there is an indication that a soul saving revelation needs to be imparted to them that will deliver their souls out of the heaviness of temptation they are experiencing. When the revelation comes, Peter says a visitation from God will be evident in the physical realm that will be witnessed even by people who do not know God and can only see in this physical realm! (See 1 Peter 2:12.) This revelation will cause the gate of the soul to open up and His will to be done on earth as it is in heaven. It is a heavenly manifestation in the earth that is brought about by the mind being saved! **Be transformed by the renewing of your mind.** (Romans 12:2)

It says in 1 Peter One, verse eight. **...you rejoice with joy inexpressible and full of glory, receiving...** Does that sound like a joy gusher released out of the spirit which brings forth the end result in the soul, a joy gusher which casts off the heaviness? Grief cannot sustain an attack against the joy of the Lord. When heaviness is coming on the mind and emotions, the one thing that person does not 'feel' like doing is rejoicing. But when you realize this is the event for which you have been practicing and now you have located the enemy's position, this is the result of your mind being renewed, this is the home stretch, you expectantly 'prime the pump' with rejoicing. **Again I will say, rejoice...the Lord is at hand.** (Philippians 4:4-5) As you continue to rejoice in the Lord, that gusher on the inside is released and you find yourself rejoicing with Joy unspeakable and full of the glory of God. The glory of the Father is what (Who) raised Jesus from the dead (Romans 6:4). It's the resurrection power of God that will give life to any dead situation. Jesus said, **All things are possible to him who believes.** (Mark 9:23) And **Thy will be done on earth as it is in heaven.** (Matthew 6:10) Can you see the potential of this revelation when the Body of Christ really understands and applies itself to the salvation of the soul?

I have released to you just a taste of this revelation of soul salvation. Study it yourself and apply yourself to see it work in your own life. Don't ever quit. This is a race that is not over until <u>you</u> say it is over. **If God is for us who can be against us.** (Romans 8:31)

Dr. Elizabeth Smither was a practicing veterinarian for twenty years before she was called into full time ministry. She is presently the assistant pastor of Grace Fellowship world distribution Center in Frankfort, Kentucky. Her teaching gift has been in the area of soul restoration. Seeing the Body of Christ develop into the maturity that is available is her vision.